CRIME FILES

Written by Jane Langford

Contents

How to Read the Plays

There are three plays in this book for you to read aloud in a small group. There are six characters in each play.

1   Choose a character.

2   Look through the play at your character's lines.

3   Read your lines quietly to yourself.

4   Read the whole play aloud in your group.

Reading tips

• Follow the play carefully, even when it is not your turn to read.

• Read your lines clearly.

• Try to speak in the way your character would. If you think your character is loud and bossy, then read your part in a loud, bossy voice.

The Getaway

A Play by Jane Langford

Illustrations by Nick Spender

Cast

Paul

Elliot

Butch

Chad

Sal

Griffin

The Getaway

Act 1
4.15 pm, dusk, on a country road

Two boys are walking home from school. A car is being driven at high speed. Suddenly, there is a screech of brakes and a thud.

Griffin You hit something!

Sal No, I didn't.

Griffin Yes, you did. Stop!

Chad Are you joking? We're on the run. We can't stop for anything.

Griffin But the car hit something.

Butch Who cares? Those guards back at the prison won't stay asleep for ever – not even with what *we* put in their tea!

Sal And when they do wake up, the police will soon be after us.

Chad Yeah! Police forces from the whole of Britain will be chasing us!

Butch There'll be warnings sent to all the ports and airports.

Chad So we'd better get to the airport before they do. *(Taps Sal on the shoulder)* Put your foot down on that accelerator, Sal.

Griffin NO! YOU CAN'T! I know you hit something! … I think it was a boy!

Chad *(Shocked)* A boy?

Griffin *(Urgently)* Yes! A boy! Now stop the car and back up!

The car screeches to a halt, then reverses aggressively back up the lane.

Chad *(Horrified)* It's not one boy! It's two!

Butch Are they dead?

Sal No. One of them is getting up. He's a bit wobbly on his feet, but he looks OK.

Griffin What about the other one?

Sal I don't know.

*Everyone in the car is quiet. They watch the boys,
hoping the second boy will get up. Nothing happens.*

Paul   Elliot! *(Leans over Elliot and shakes him)*
Elliot! Are you all right?

Elliot   *(Groans)* No … it hurts … *(Eyes flutter
open)* What happened?

Paul   That car! It hit us! It came flying out
of nowhere.

Elliot   *(Groans)* How fast was it going?

Paul   I don't know. Look! You're bleeding!

Elliot   I know. It's my leg. It really hurts.

Paul   Don't worry. I'll get help.

Paul runs towards the car, waving his arms. Griffin jumps out of the car and walks over to meet him. The rest of the gang follow.

Paul   Help! Help! My friend's hurt!

Griffin   Let me see … *(Bends over Elliot)* Are you all right, lad?

Elliot   No! It hurts. I can't move my leg.

Griffin tears Elliot's trouser leg and looks at his injured leg.

Griffin   It's really smashed up. We'll have to get you to hospital.

Sal   No! … No hospital!

Griffin   But you can't leave him here.

Sal   Can't I? You just watch me!

Sal turns to walk away and motions to the rest of the gang to follow her. Griffin catches hold of her arm.

Griffin Stop! OK – we won't take him to hospital. But we have to get him somewhere safe and warm, then call for help.

Sal Like where?

Chad We passed a farmhouse up the road. It looked empty. Perhaps the owners are away. We could break in and hide there while we decide what to do.

Sal And it might have a phone. OK, we'll let the boy make one phone call, then we're out of here!

Act 2

6.00 pm, at the empty farmhouse

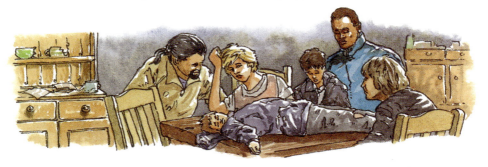

*Everyone is gathered around the kitchen table,
looking at Elliot, who is lying on it.*

Elliot *(Tries to sit up)* Help me! It hurts!

Paul Lie back down! I'll call for the ambulance.

Butch No, wait.

Paul What do you mean … wait?

Butch Just what I said – WAIT!

Elliot Paul, I feel terrible. Please get some help.

Sal *(Ignores Elliot and looks at Butch)*
What's wrong?

Butch   We've wasted a lot of time. What if the police are already after us? What if they're setting up road blocks right now?

Sal   Then let's dump the kids and get to the airport, quick!

Butch   Hold on a minute. Let's think about this. We can't risk getting caught again.

Sal   So … what do we do?

Butch   Nothing. Just sit tight. We can stay here until everything blows over. *(Looks around and peers in the cupboards)* There's enough food and it's warm.

Griffin   But what about the lads?

Chad   What about them?

Paul   *(Urgently)* Elliot needs help. He's hurt. YOU hurt him. I'm going to call the police.

Chad *(Rips phone out of wall)* No, you're not!

Paul *(To the gang, accusingly)* What's going on? Who are you? What have you done?

Chad What have we done! I'll tell you what we've done. We've done five long years in prison and we're not doing a minute longer. Sal was our getaway driver before we were caught. She helped us break out of prison and we're not going back – not for anyone.

Griffin   But the lad is hurt. We have to get help.

Sal   No. We don't have to. If it wasn't for you we'd be at the airport by now.

Griffin   I didn't run the kids over!

Butch   No. But you made us stop. Now shut up and make us something to eat.

Griffin retreats to the far end of the kitchen.
Paul follows him. They speak in hushed whispers.

Paul   Have you really escaped from prison?

Griffin   Yes.

Paul   Were you in for murder?

Griffin   No, armed robbery.

Paul   If Elliot dies, it will be murder. He's lost a lot of blood. He needs to go to hospital.

Griffin   I know. I've tried to tell the others but they won't listen. I can't help you.

Paul   You have to. Elliot mustn't die.

Sal   Hey! You two! What are you whispering about? Get back down here with that food.

Paul   (*Urgently*) Please! Please help me!

Griffin is unsure. He looks at Elliot. Elliot groans.

Elliot   Paul, where are you? Is the ambulance coming?

Paul   Please! He could die!

Griffin   OK … I'll find a way to help. But keep your mouth shut for now!

Act 3

10.30 pm, at the empty farmhouse

Griffin is pacing anxiously up and down the kitchen.

Paul   Elliot is getting worse.

Elliot   Is that you, Dad?

Paul   No. It's me, Paul.

Elliot   I'm sorry I'm late, Dad. I didn't mean to make you cross.

Paul   I'm not cross and I'm not your dad! I'm Paul.

Elliot   Is Mum there? I don't feel very well.

Paul   What's wrong with him? He's talking nonsense.

Griffin Sometimes people talk nonsense when they're badly hurt.

Paul Please! We have to go and get help!

Chad We're not going anywhere. We're staying here till the heat is off. Now sit down and shut up or I'll belt you!

Griffin Don't do that! Look, why don't I take him out of everybody's way? There's a sofa in the living room. He could lie down on that and get a few hours' sleep.

Paul Sleep? Are you mad? I don't want to sleep!

Griffin glares meaningfully at Paul.

Chad You'll do as you're told! Now go into the living room and give us all some peace.

Elliot Don't go! Don't go!

Griffin marches Paul into the living room.

Griffin (*Loudly, so the rest of the gang can hear*) Lie down there and go to sleep.

Griffin puts his finger to his lips to shush Paul, then motions for Paul to follow him.

Paul (*Whispering*) What are you doing?

Griffin Letting you go. Climb out of this window, then make a run for it.

Griffin opens a window and helps Paul onto the sill.

Griffin Do you know where to go?

Paul Yes. If I turn right at the end of the lane, I should be home in fifteen minutes.

Griffin Good. I'll give you a ten-minute start, then I'm going to get the others out of here before the police come. We'll just have to take our chances with the road blocks.

Paul   Thank you.

Griffin   That's OK. I couldn't let the lad suffer any longer. I've got a lad of my own about the same age. I've barely seen him since I've been in prison.

Paul   I'm sorry.

Griffin   Don't be sorry, it's my own fault. Just get out of here. Quick! Before the others come.

Paul slips silently out of the window and runs off into the night. Griffin shuts the window behind him. It creaks noisily.

Sal   What was that noise?

Chad   I don't know. I didn't hear anything.

Butch   I did. *(Stands up and looks towards the living room)* Is everything all right in there?

Griffin   Yes, fine. The lad's going off to sleep.

Butch walks into the living room. He sees that Paul has gone.

Butch   Where is he?

Griffin   *(Nervously)* He's gone.

Butch *(Shouting angrily)* I can see that. But where has he gone?

Griffin I've let him go.

The rest of the gang rush into the living room.

Sal *(Disbelieving)* You've let him go?

Chad Why have you let him go?

Griffin You know why. I couldn't let that lad in there die. *(Marches back to the kitchen)* Look at him!

Elliot *(Weakly)* Help me! Mum! Dad!

Butch You stupid fool! The police will be searching the lanes for the missing lads. They've probably got the place surrounded by now! We're all going to go back to prison and it's your fault!

Butch lunges at Griffin as if he is about to kill him.

A siren wails. The police and Paul burst in through the door.

Paul   *(Shouting)* STOP! Leave him alone!

Butch is stunned. He stands still and the police grab him.

Griffin   *(Smiles at Paul)* Thank you.

Paul   *(To Griffin)* I'm sorry I didn't give you time to get away. The police were out looking for Elliot and me. They picked me up at the end of the lane.

Griffin   It doesn't matter. You had to save your friend … and you've done me a favour really.

Tom How?

Griffin Well, if I'd escaped I would have always been on the run. I'd never have been able to go home to see my lad. This way I'll have to serve the rest of my time, but when they let me out, I can make a fresh start. So, like I said, thanks.

Paul smiles and goes over to Elliot who is looking around.

Elliot Is everything going to be all right now?

Paul Yes! Everything is going to be fine.

Hostages

A Play by Jane Langford
Illustrations by Kaye Hodges

Cast

Blake

Ray

Mr Chadwick

Mrs Chadwick

Jane

Scott

Hostages

Act 1

Late afternoon, Mr and Mrs Chadwick's home

Ray Hurry up! Knock on the door!

Blake Calm down! No one has seen us.

Ray They will if we hang around here much longer.

Blake OK. Here goes.

Blake knocks on the door.
Mrs Chadwick opens it.

Mrs Chadwick Hello, can I help you?

Ray Yes. *(Pushes Mrs Chadwick back into the hall)*. Get in there and shut up!

Mrs Chadwick *(Shocked)* No! Stop! What are you doing? What do you want?

Blake   Shut up! No more questions. We ask the questions from now on.

Ray   Yes. Like … is there anyone else here apart from you and the kids?

Mrs Chadwick   Yes, my husband is here.

Blake   Nice try, lady. But you're lying. Your husband is at work. We trailed him to the bank this morning.

Mrs Chadwick   What? You trailed him? Why?

Blake   I told you, we ask the questions from now on. Get in the living room and shut up!

Mrs Chadwick But the children are in there.
I'm not letting you go in there to
upset them.

Ray You're not letting me? I'm not giving
you a choice. Now MOVE! *(Pushes
Mrs Chadwick into the living room)*

Jane Mum! What's going on?

Mrs Chadwick Don't worry, Jane. Everything is
all right.

Scott But who are these men?
Where's Dad?

Mrs Chadwick He'll be home soon. Now you two
go upstairs while I talk to these men.

Blake *(Blocks the doorway)* You two are
not going anywhere! You're going
to stay here where we can keep an
eye on you.

Jane   Mum? Who are these men?

Scott   *(Frightened)* I want Dad!

Mrs Chadwick   Just sit down and be quiet while I talk to these gentlemen.

Ray   We're not gentlemen …

Blake   … and we didn't come here to talk. We've got quite a different plan in mind. Your husband is going to unlock the safe at the bank and give us all the money.

Mrs Chadwick   He'll never do that!

Blake   I think he will when he sees what we might do to his children.

Ray   NOW SIT DOWN! *(Points to chair by table)* Put your hands behind your back!

Mrs Chadwick   *(Panicking)* What are you going to do?

Ray   Shut up! *(To Blake)* Get the rope out of the bag, Blake. Tie her up!

Jane   No! You can't do that!

As Blake ties up Mrs Chadwick, the telephone rings.

Blake   *(Jumps and looks startled)* Who's that?

Mrs Chadwick   It's probably my husband. He rings to see if I need anything from the shops when he comes home from work.

Blake   *(Firmly)* Speak to him. But don't say anything silly.

Ray   *(Grabs Scott)* Or this kid won't ever talk again!

Mrs Chadwick   Hello.

Mr Chadwick   Hello, dear. Everything all right?

Mrs Chadwick (*Voice trembling*) Yes, fine.

Mr Chadwick I'm on my way home. Do you want anything from the shops?

Mrs Chadwick Um, yes, please. Can you get me a loaf of bread?

Mr Chadwick Bread?

Mrs Chadwick Yes, please – a loaf of bread. We haven't got any left.

Mr Chadwick (*Surprised*) You're sure you need some bread? OK, I'll see you in half an hour. Bye.

Mrs Chadwick Bye. (*To Ray*) Take your hands off my son!

Ray Don't worry, I will. But first he's going to be tied up, just like you!

Ray and Blake tie Scott and Jane to chairs.

Act 2

Later that evening, Mr and Mrs Chadwick's home

Mr Chadwick Hello, everybody! I'm home!

Scott DAD! DON'T COME IN!

Jane GET THE POLICE! QUICK! RUN!

Mr Chadwick Scott? Jane? What's wrong?
(*Rushes into living room*)

Ray (*Chuckles unpleasantly*) Nothing's wrong. Everything is just fine now that you're here.

Mr Chadwick What are you doing here? What have you done to my family?

Ray Er … your family. What can I say? *(Grins cruelly)* They're just a bit tied up at the moment.

Mr Chadwick *(Angrily)* You thugs! Untie them at once!

Blake Untie them? But that isn't part of the plan.

Mr Chadwick Plan? What are you talking about?

Jane Dad, they want you to open up the bank, unlock the safe, and steal all the money for them.

Scott Don't do it, Dad!

Mr Chadwick What? Open up the bank? Unlock the safe? Is this right?

Mrs Chadwick *(Voice shaking)* Yes. They are going to keep us here as hostages until you take them to get the money.

Mr Chadwick But that's impossible. I can't reopen the bank tonight. The central alarm system has been set. If I tamper with it, I will trigger the alarm and the police will descend on the place in seconds.

Blake *(Calmly)* So when can you open the bank?

Mr Chadwick Not until 8 o'clock in the morning.

Blake *(Nods contentedly)* That's what we thought. So we'll spend a quiet evening together, then in the morning …

Ray … YOU'LL GET US THE CASH!

Mr Chadwick No, I can't do it!

Blake Can't?

Ray Or won't?

Mr Chadwick I can't. The assistant manager always helps me to open up. She would never agree to your plan.

Blake She doesn't have to agree. All she has to do is shut up!

Ray Or we'll shut her up for good!

Scott (*Blinking back tears*) Dad! They can't do that!

Mr Chadwick Don't worry, Scott. Everything will be fine.

Blake   That's right. Everything will be OK as long as your dad behaves himself.

Scott   I hate you! I'm going to call the police as soon as you've gone.

Ray   You won't get a chance! We'll leave you safely bound and gagged.

Blake   You won't be able to move a muscle. You'll all stay exactly where you are.

Mrs Chadwick   You can't leave us tied up like this. You can't be serious?

Blake   I'm deadly serious, Mrs Chadwick.
When we set off for the bank in the
morning, none of you will be going
anywhere. And if you try anything
foolish …

Ray   … don't forget that we've got
your husband.

Mrs Chadwick   You can't threaten us like this.

Blake   Can't we? Just you wait and see.

*Ray grabs Mr Chadwick and ties him up next to his
wife and children.*

Act 3

The next morning, inside the bank

Blake Hurry up! Put the gag on that assistant manager and come and help me.

Ray I'm coming. I just had to make sure she was tied up properly. She put up a bit of a struggle.

Blake Oh did she? Well that's funny, Mr Chadwick is having a bit of a *struggle* with his memory. He's forgotten the security code that will unlock the safe.

Ray I'm sure I can help him to remember. *(Grabs Mr Chadwick threateningly)* Or perhaps I should go home and ask his wife?

Mr Chadwick No! Don't do that!

Blake So let's open the safe and stop messing about.

Mr Chadwick keys in the security code and unlocks the safe.

Mr Chadwick There! It's unlocked. Take the money! Take as much as you want. But it won't do you any good.

Blake Really? Why not?

Mr Chadwick You're not quite as clever as you think. The police are here. They've surrounded the bank. There's no way for you to escape.

Ray   Oh, yes. What a joker!

Mr Chadwick   I'm not joking. I contacted the police before I came home last night. I knew there was something wrong as soon as I heard my wife on the phone.

Blake   What do you mean you knew something was wrong? She hardly said anything to you.

Mr Chadwick   I could tell something was wrong from the tone of her voice. Also, she asked me to get a loaf of bread.

Blake   So what?

Mr Chadwick   We went to the supermarket at the weekend. We bought enough bread to feed an army for a fortnight. I knew she was trying to let me know something was wrong.

Ray You're lying. If the police had known about us, they would have come to the house last night.

Mr Chadwick No, they wouldn't. It was too dangerous. I didn't know what was happening and I wasn't prepared to risk my family's safety.

Blake So how do you know the police are here now?

Mr Chadwick They're bound to be. I was fitted with a hidden microphone before I came into the house last night. The police know exactly where we are and everything we've been saying.

Ray (*Threateningly*) I'll get you for this!

The police burst into the bank, grab Ray and Blake and take them away.

A relieved Mr Chadwick reaches for the phone and rings home.

Scott   *(Picks up phone)* Hello.

Mr Chadwick   Scott! Are you all right, Son?

Scott   Yes. *(To Mrs Chadwick and Jane)* It's Dad!

Mr Chadwick   Is Jane all right?

Scott   Yes. Here she is. *(Passes phone to Jane)*

Jane   Dad! Dad!

Mr Chadwick   Hello, Jane.

Jane   Hello, Dad! The police are here! They rescued us as soon as you left. *(To Mrs Chadwick)* Mum, come and talk to Dad. *(Passes phone to Mrs Chadwick)*

Mrs Chadwick   *(Relieved)* Hello! I'm so glad you're all right. Will you be back soon?

Mr Chadwick   Of course.

Mrs Chadwick   There's just one thing.

Mr Chadwick   What's that?

Mrs Chadwick   Could you bring a loaf of bread?

Mr Chadwick   What?

Mrs Chadwick   You see, I've made so many sandwiches for the police, there really *isn't* any bread left!

Snatched!

A Play by Jane Langford
Illustrations by Biz Hull

Cast

Mr Roberts

Jake

Dr Oliver

Nurse

Stranger

Detective Inspector Jones

Snatched!

Act 1
The Reception area of a busy hospital

Mr Roberts and Jake enter.

Dr Oliver   *(Strides forward to shake hands)*
Mr Roberts! Jake! It's good to meet
you again. Let's hope this operation
on Jake's eyes will be the last.

Mr Roberts   Yes, we certainly hope so.

Dr Oliver   Could you come into my office for a
quick word, Mr Roberts?

*Mr Roberts and Dr Oliver go into a nearby office
while Jake waits outside.*

Dr Oliver   Has Jake's sight been any better since the last operation?

Mr Roberts   Yes. There's been a big improvement, but he still says everything's fuzzy and unfocused.

Dr Oliver   Well, I'm hoping that this next operation will make all the difference, but you know it's risky, don't you?

Mr Roberts   Yes, I know, but Jake's desperate to see properly again. Things haven't been easy for him since the car accident.

Outside the office, a stranger has approached Jake.

Stranger   Hello, Jake.

Jake   *(Puzzled)* Hello. I'm sorry, your voice sounds familiar but I can't see very well. Do I know you?

Stranger *(Coughs and lowers voice)* You did know me, Jake ... once upon a time.

Jake *(Uncomfortable)* Did I? When?

Stranger Oh, a long time ago. And I knew your father as well. He's a very rich man isn't he, Jake? It doesn't seem fair does it – that some men can have so much and others so little?

Jake Um – I suppose not. Does my dad owe you money?

Stranger Oh yes, he owes me all right. *(Grabs Jake's arm)* And he's going to pay dearly to get his precious son back!

Jake *(Pulling away)* Get off! Leave me alone!

Nurse Hey! What's going on? What are you doing with that boy?

Stranger None of your business, lady. Now stay out of the way!

Nurse Stop! Leave the boy alone! You're not going to take him anywhere.

Stranger Oh, yes I am. *(Pulls Jake towards the door and pushes the nurse aside)*

Nurse *(Shouting)* Dr Oliver! Dr Oliver!

Dr Oliver runs out of his office.

Dr Oliver What's going on?

Nurse Quick, a man has got hold of that boy! He's trying to abduct him!

Dr Oliver I'll stop him! You call the police.

Dr Oliver launches himself at the stranger. The stranger lets go of Jake and escapes through the door.

Mr Roberts *(Rushes out of office)* What's going on? Where's Jake?

Jake Dad! I'm here! A man tried to grab me. He said you owed him something.

Mr Roberts *(Hugs Jake closely)* Owed him something? What did he mean?

Jake I don't know.

Mr Roberts Well, thank goodness you're safe. Did he hurt you?

Jake No. I'm all right.

Mr Roberts   Has anyone called the police?

Dr Oliver   Yes, don't worry. They're on their way.
Let's go into my office and sit down.

*Five minutes later, the police arrive. Some search the
grounds for the stranger, while D.I. Jones goes into
Dr Oliver's office.*

D.I. Jones   What's been happening here, then?

Mr Roberts   *(Upset)* Someone tried to snatch
my son.

Nurse   I saw what happened. A man caught hold of the boy's arm and tried to pull him out of the main door.

D.I. Jones   What did this man look like?

Nurse   I don't know. It happened so fast. He was tall and wearing jeans. That's all I noticed.

D.I. Jones   And you, son? Did you see his face clearly?

Jake   No, not clearly. I can't see anything clearly.

Mr Roberts   *(Impatiently)* Look, what are you going to do to protect my son?

D.I. Jones   Don't worry, Sir. I'll arrange for a police guard to protect your son day and night. In the meantime, we'll try to find out what this is all about.

Act 2

The next day, in a private hospital room

D.I. Jones is sitting in the corner. Mr Roberts and the nurse are by Jake's bed. The phone rings and the nurse answers it.

Nurse Hello.

Stranger Hello. Can I speak to Mr Roberts, please?

Nurse Oh, yes of course. *(Hands phone to Mr Roberts)* It's for you.

Mr Roberts Hello.

Stranger *(Deliberately disguising voice)* Hello, Mr Roberts. I think it's time we came to some agreement about that boy of yours.

Mr Roberts What are you talking about? Who is this?

Mr Roberts signals urgently to D.I. Jones.
Dr Oliver enters.

D.I. Jones   *(Whispering)* Who is it?

Mr Roberts   *(Cups hand over phone)* That man –
the one who tried to snatch Jake.

D.I. Jones   *(Talking into police radio handset)* Put a
trace on the phone in Room 301.
It's the kidnapper!

Stranger   It's simple. You pay me £100,000 and
your son stays alive. What do you say?

Mr Roberts   You'll never get near my son again.
There's a police guard on his room.

D.I. Jones   *(Whispering to Mr Roberts)* Keep him
talking! We need time to trace the call.

Stranger   How can you be so sure I won't get your son? Not even the police can watch someone every moment of the day and night. Anyway, why risk it? Give me £100,000 and I'll leave your son alone.

Mr Roberts   *(Angrily)* I don't care what threats you make. You won't get any money out of me!

Stranger   Really, Mr Roberts? In that case I will just have to pay another visit to your son.

Mr Roberts   What? You wouldn't dare! …
Hello … Hello

The line goes dead. Mr Roberts slams down the phone.

D.I. Jones   I told you to keep him talking.

Mr Roberts   I tried, but he hung up. Have you got a trace?

D.I. Jones *(Shakes head)* No. There wasn't time.

Mr Roberts Now what do we do?

D.I. Jones We need to catch this man and fast.
Are you sure you can't remember
anything else about him, Jake?

Jake *(Shakes head)* No ... nothing ...
except perhaps the way he smells.
I think it's aftershave. It's very strong
and I'm sure I've smelt it before
somewhere.

D.I. Jones Where?

Jake I don't know. I can't remember ...
He said he knew me and his voice
seemed familiar too, but ...

D.I. Jones Come on, Jake. Try. This is very
important. Where do you think you've
met this man before?

Jake   *(Tearfully)* I don't know. I told you,
I can't remember.

Dr Oliver   Never mind, Jake. You mustn't worry
about that any more now. You're
going to have your operation soon.
I'm going to give you some medicine
to make you sleep.

Jake   But what about that man?

Nurse   Don't worry about him. Now … ssh …
just relax.

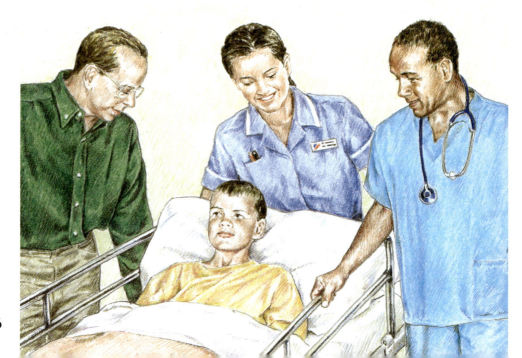

Jake gradually falls asleep.

D.I. Jones If only Jake could remember where he's smelt that smell before.

Mr Roberts Yes, but he's had trouble remembering things ever since the car crash.

D.I. Jones Really? How exactly did the crash happen?

Mr Roberts My driver was late driving him to school. He was always late. That day he overtook on a corner. He hit another car, injuring the driver and blinding my son.

Dr Oliver It was a terrible thing to happen, but at least we're giving him a chance of seeing again with this operation. Come on, let's take him to the operating theatre.

Act 3

Several days later, in the private hospital room

Jake is asleep in bed with bandages round his eyes.

D.I. Jones How is he today?

Nurse He's doing very well. We're going to take his bandages off this morning.

Jake *(Wakes up)* Dad?

Mr Roberts I'm here, Jake.

Jake I'm scared. What if the operation hasn't worked?

Mr Roberts We have to hope that it has, Jake. Be brave.

Dr Oliver Come on, young man. Sit up. Let me take those bandages off you. *(Unwraps bandages)* There – how's that?

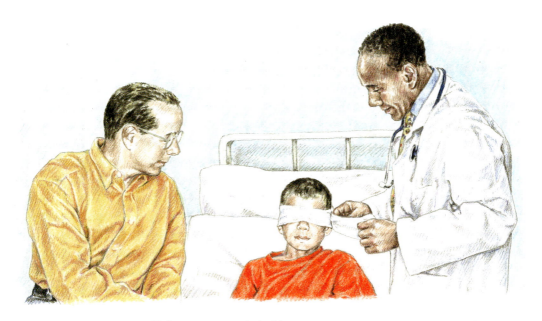

Jake *(Uncertainly)* I'm not sure … It's still a
bit fuzzy. *(Blinks)*

Mr Roberts Oh no!

Jake *(Excitedly)* No! Dad, I can see you.
I can. I can see!

*Mr Roberts hugs Jake. They talk for a while and then
Dr Oliver examines Jake's eyes carefully.*

Dr Oliver Good. It looks like the operation has
been a complete success.

Jake Great! Can I go home now?

Dr Oliver   Yes, of course. If you come with me, Mr Roberts, to sign some papers, you can ring for a taxi at the same time.

Mr Roberts   That would be perfect.

Nurse   I'll get a porter to take Jake to the taxi when it arrives.

Dr Oliver, Mr Roberts and the nurse exit.

D.I. Jones   Well, Jake. You can see again and you're going home! That calls for a celebration. *(Gives Jake some of his chocolate bar)* Here, have some chocolate!

Jake   *(Chuckles)* Thanks!

The stranger enters disguised as a porter. He is pushing an empty wheelchair.

D.I. Jones   Oh! Here's the porter to take you to your taxi … hop in!

The stranger starts to push Jake out of the room.

Jake   Shouldn't we wait for Dad?

Stranger   *(Gruffly)* He's just in the corridor.
Let's go and find him.

Jake   OK … *(To D.I. Jones)* Bye. Thanks for
looking after me.

D.I. Jones   That's all right, Jake. Here – you'd
better have the rest of this chocolate –
it'll only make me fat!

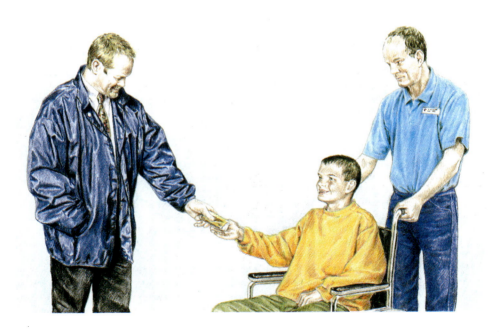

61

Jake takes the chocolate, but drops it. The stranger bends over Jake to pick it up. Jake sniffs the air suspiciously.

Jake   Wait! Um … I've forgotten my bag. Can you get it for me?

Stranger   One of the nurses can get it.

Jake   No! I want it now!

The stranger grumbles, but goes across the room to fetch the bag.

Jake   (Whispering) Inspector, it's *him*!

D.I. Jones   Who? The porter?

Jake   Yes! It's the same smell – the aftershave. I smelt it when he bent over me … and there's something else. I know this man. I'm sure I do.

Stranger   Here's your bag. Now let's go.

Jake No! You're the one who tried to snatch me.

Stranger What are you talking about? I'm a porter.

The stranger grabs the wheelchair and quickly pushes Jake towards the door.

D.I. Jones Stop! Stand still! You're under arrest! *(Grabs stranger and puts on handcuffs)* Well done, Jake. You handled that well.

Jake I know who he is! I remember! He's Baxter!

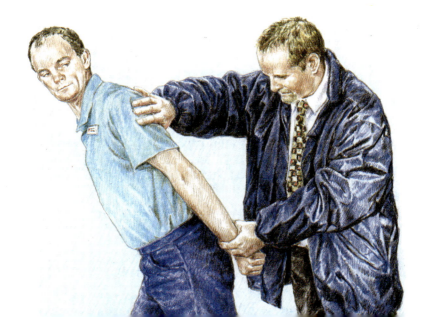

Mr Roberts enters.

Mr Roberts That's Baxter!

D.I. Jones Who's Baxter?

Mr Roberts Baxter is the driver who caused Jake's accident. He was charged with dangerous driving and he got three months in prison. I made sure he would never get a job as a driver again.

Stranger And I've never had a job since. You've ruined my life!

D.I. Jones *(Marches Baxter out of the room)* You're coming to the police station with me!

Jake No! Wait! I want to look at him. I want to be sure that I never forget his face.